POLLINATOR PARTNERSHIP ACTION PLAN

Pollinator Health Task Force

JUNE 2016

June 22, 2016

On behalf of the Pollinator Health Task Force, we are pleased to transmit the *Pollinator Partnership Action Plan* (PPAP). The PPAP responds to the President's emphasis on public-private partnerships in his June 2014 Memorandum "Creating a Federal Strategy to Promote the Health of Honey Bees and Other Pollinators." This special focus on partnerships was reiterated in the Federal Pollinator Strategy commitment to prepare a Partnership Action Plan to amplify the many Federal actions advanced under the Presidential Memorandum through complementary state and private-sector actions. Only through such coordinated national efforts can we expeditiously expand pollinator-health initiatives to achieve the scale necessary to make meaningful and long-term improvements. In particular, Federal agencies are working with the private sector toward ways to institutionalize these changes into business models and public understanding. This reflects the growing understanding of the ecological services provided to humanity by pollinators, and the importance of all lands—even those on the margins—to providing habitat and forage for these creatures.

Hon. Tom Vilsack
Secretary of Agriculture

Hon. Gina McCarthy
Administrator, U.S. Environmental Protection Agency

Contents

Executive Summary

Bees, birds, butterflies, bats, and other animals provide pollination services that are essential to the survival of flowering plants, and in doing so underpin the diverse ecosystems and agricultural productivity on which humanity depends. Pollinators are responsible for one in every three bites of food we take, with honey bees alone increasing our nation's crop values by more than 15 billion dollars each year. Many pollinators are in serious decline in the United States and worldwide.[1] Responding to these declines, in June 2014 President Obama issued a Presidential Memorandum[2] establishing the Pollinator Health Task Force (Task Force), a Federal interagency body charged with coordinating Federal efforts to promote pollinator health through research, habitat creation, education and outreach, and public-private partnerships. In May 2015, the Task Force released its national *Strategy to Promote the Health of Honey Bees and Other Pollinators* and accompanying *Pollinator Research Action Plan,*[3] outlining needs and priority actions to better understand pollinator losses and improve pollinator health. In particular, these documents outlined three overarching goals for pollinator health in the United States, summarized as:

1. Reduce honey bee overwintering colony losses to no more than 15% within 10 years;

2. Increase the Eastern population of the monarch butterfly to cover approximately 15 acres in the overwintering grounds in Mexico; and,

3. Restore or enhance 7 million acres of land for pollinators over the next 5 years.

Achieving these goals will require an "all hands on deck" approach that harnesses the expertise and capabilities of the Federal government, in collaboration with: state, local, and tribal governments; the private, academic, and non-profit sectors; and the general public. Recognizing this broad need, and in response to a directive in the aforementioned Presidential Memorandum, this *Pollinator Partnership Action Plan* (PPAP) provides examples of successful past and ongoing collaborations between the Federal government and non-Federal institutions to support pollinator health under each of the above goals. It also highlights areas that are ripe for future collaboration. The primary audiences for the PPAP are state and local governments, private companies, universities, community organizations, and other entities that organize and/or represent citizen stakeholders and have the resources needed to implement and support collaborative efforts with Federal agencies.

Importantly, the PPAP is not an exhaustive listing of existing[4] and possible public-private collaborations, but rather provides a demonstrative sampling of how such collaborations can enhance and accelerate pollinator-health efforts, and build the support necessary to sustain improvements in pollinator health over the long term. A key takeaway is that the exact nature of public-private collaborations can and should take many forms, depending on the particular circumstances of the region targeted and the institutions and populations engaged. Indeed, national enthusiasm and engagement on pollinator health

---

1. http://www.ipbes.net/sites/default/files/downloads/Pollination_Summary%20for%20policymakers_EN_.pdf
2. https://www.whitehouse.gov/the-press-office/2014/06/20/presidential-memorandum-creating-federal-strategy-promote-health-honey-b
3. https://www.whitehouse.gov/blog/2015/05/19/announcing-new-steps-promote-pollinator-health
4. See Appendix A of the Pollinator Research Action Plan for a more extensive list of Web Sites with Resources and Tools for Pollinator Health. https://www.whitehouse.gov/sites/default/files/microsites/ostp/Pollinator%20Research%20Action%20Plan%202015.pdf

in response to the President's leadership and call to action in this area has already motivated a wide range of activities: from schoolchildren planting gardens for the Million Pollinator Garden Challenge; to corporate support for pollinator habitat on business and agricultural lands; to Federal, interstate, and private actions to improve habitat on transportation, powerline, and other rights-of-way. The PPAP seeks to celebrate and lift up these and other collaborative activities as models for future efforts, and to encourage ideas for new and creative ways to engage all sectors in protecting the pollinators on which we all depend.

Introduction

Pollinators are integral parts of managed and natural ecosystems, providing billions of dollars in pollination services. Today, pollinators face a variety of challenges, including habitat loss due to development, altered land use patterns, and climate change, as well as exposure to pests, pathogens, pesticides, and other stressors. At the direction of President Obama in the 2014 "Presidential Memorandum—Creating a Federal Strategy to Promote the Health of Honey Bees and Other Pollinators", the Federal Pollinator Health Task Force (Task Force) developed the *Strategy to Promote the Health of Honey Bees and Other Pollinators* (Strategy). The Strategy, released in May 2015, describes needs and priority actions to better understand pollinator losses and improve the health of pollinators in the United States, including honey bees and native pollinators. The Strategy focuses on three overarching goals:

1. **Honey Bees:** Reduce honey bee colony losses during winter (overwintering mortality) to no more than 15% within 10 years. This goal is informed by the previously released Bee Informed Partnership surveys and the newly established quarterly and annual surveys by the USDA National Agricultural Statistics Service. Based on the robust data anticipated from the national, statistically-based NASS surveys of beekeepers, the Task Force will develop baseline data and additional goal metrics for winter, summer, and total annual colony loss.

2. **Monarch Butterflies:** Increase the Eastern population of the monarch butterfly to 225 million butterflies occupying an area of approximately 15 acres (6 hectares) in the overwintering grounds in Mexico, through domestic/international actions and public-private partnerships, by 2020.

3. **Pollinator Habitat Acreage:** Restore or enhance 7 million acres of land for pollinators over the next 5 years through Federal actions and public/private partnerships.

To support actions to achieve these goals, the Task Force developed a *Pollinator Research Action Plan* designed to focus Federal efforts on producing the scientific information needed to understand, minimize, and recover from pollinator losses. Task Force agencies also developed pollinator Best Management Practice (BMP) guidance documents for designed and natural landscapes,[5] Federally-managed lands,[6] and highway roadside maintenance,[7] and landscaping standards for Federal buildings.[8]

The Federal government cannot tackle pollinator challenges alone. In conducting research, habitat restoration, policy development and implementation, and other activities to improve pollinator health, it is imperative that the Federal government leverage the unique knowledge, resources, and capabilities of state, local, and tribal governments; non-governmental organizations; academia; private industry; and individuals and communities. This *Pollinator Partnership Action Plan* (PPAP) describes ongoing Federal partnerships, and priorities for future partnerships, to support each of the three overarching goals of the Strategy—honey bees, monarch butterflies, and pollinator habitat. While the PPAP is structured to reflect

---

5. https://www.whitehouse.gov/sites/default/files/docs/supporting_the_health_of_honey_bees_and_other_pollinators.pdf

6. http://www.fs.fed.us/wildflowers/pollinators/BMPs/

7. https://www.environment.fhwa.dot.gov/ecosystems/Pollinators_Roadsides/BMPs_pollinators_roadsides.pdf

8. GSA PBS-P100 Facilities Standards for the Public Buildings Service, Section 2.5 5 http://www.gsa.gov/portal/mediald/127494/fileName/P100_2016.action

these reporting priorities, it is important to note that partnership opportunities are not limited to these three topics, either singularly or in aggregate. Partnership opportunities can advance our knowledge on the health of other pollinating insects, birds, and bats, and on ways to reverse declines. For example, the North American Pollinator Protection Campaign (NAPPC[9]) represents a diverse collaboration of private sector organizations, academia, and government agencies working to protect pollinators broadly, addressing needs related to each of these three topics, in addition to a focus on threatened species.

Definition of Partnerships

In this document, "partnership" refers broadly to a formal or informal relationship between two or more parties working cooperatively to foster mutual objectives. The 2014 Presidential Memorandum on Pollinator Health has led to an unprecedented level of Federal cooperation around the objective of improving pollinator health, both by establishing the interagency Federal Pollinator Health Task Force and by motivating the creation of additional intra- and interagency working groups and coordinating mechanisms.

Federal agencies have also increasingly turned to public-private partnerships to accomplish goals related to pollinator health. Each Federal agency has a specific definition of partnerships tailored to its particular mission and authorities, but generally, public-private partnerships are relationships formed between one or more Federal agencies with one or more non-Federal entities to cooperatively foster attainment of mutual objectives. These relationships may be formalized through a memorandum of understanding (MOU) or similar document, allowing for greater non-Federal participation in the delivery and financing of projects, or informally to facilitate the exchange of information. Public-private partnerships allow Federal and non-Federal entities to leverage one another's resources and expertise, help ensure that the needs and perspectives of a broad range of stakeholders are taken into account, and support project longevity. This discussion of partnerships is not intended to create any additional legal obligations on behalf of the Federal government or for any other organizations mentioned in this document.

---

9. http://pollinator.org/nappc/index.html

Focus Area 1: Honey Bee Health

Introduction

Honey bees are the most important managed pollinators in the United States. The National Academy of Sciences[10] concluded that: "[h]oney bees enable the production of no fewer than 90 commercially grown crops …" as part of the large, commercial, beekeeping industry that leases honey bee colonies for pollination services in the United States. Although overall honey bee colony numbers in recent years have remained relatively stable[11] and sufficient to meet commercial pollination needs, this has come at a cost to beekeepers who must work harder to counter increasing colony mortality rates. The exact causes for honey bee colony mortality remain an active area of research. Researchers generally believe that honey bees, like many other pollinators, are adversely impacted by a number of stressors, acting individually and in concert with one another, including habitat loss from development and changes in land use, exposure to arthropod pests, pathogens, and pesticides, in addition to frequent, long-distance, transportation of hives. Federal partnerships can help advance understanding of the mechanisms behind honey bee colony mortality, as well as application of current knowledge to reduce and reverse these losses.

Past and Ongoing Partnerships

Federal partnerships have already been established to address numerous dimensions of honey bee health, including research and development, monitoring, risk assessment and management, floral resources, and communication. Examples of past and ongoing Federal partnerships in these areas are provided below.

Research

The U.S. Department of Agriculture (USDA) supports the majority of its honey bee research through its in-house research arm, the Agricultural Research Service (ARS), and competitive grants administered by the National Institute of Food and Agriculture (NIFA). ARS has five dedicated bee research laboratories (in Baton Rouge, LA; Beltsville, MD; Davis, CA; Logan, UT; and Tucson, AZ), four of which focus on honey bees. Several other ARS laboratories also have strong bee-research programs. A variety of legal mechanisms allow ARS laboratories to enter into formal agreements with non-Federal entities, including industry, universities, and non-governmental organizations (Table 1), with similar mechanisms available to other Federal agencies.

---

10. NRC 2007. Status of Pollinators in North America. http://www.nap.edu/catalog/11761/status-of-pollinators-in-north-america

11. NASS 2016 data provide evidence of an ~8% decline in national commercial bee hive colony numbers from January 2015 – January 2016. Since this is the first year of enhanced NASS data collection it is not possible to draw trend conclusions, albeit these data warrant close monitoring. https://www.nass.usda.gov/Surveys/Guide_to_NASS_Surveys/Bee_and_Honey/

Table 1: Types of Grants and Agreements used by the Agricultural Research Service[12]

	Purpose	Relationship / Benefit to Government	Involvement of Government
Contract	Acquiring Service or Property	Direct Benefit/Use	No Involvement
Grant	Transferring Anything of Value	To Support or Stimulate a Public Purpose	No Involvement
Assistance Type Cooperative Agreement (ATCA)	Transferring Anything of Value	To Support or Stimulate a Public Purpose	Substantial Involvement
Specific Cooperative Agreement (SCA)	Agency is Paying, with Mutual Interest and Contributions toward Research Effort	Direct Benefit to Agency in-house research	Substantial Involvement
Research Support Agreement (RSA)	Procuring Service/ Supplies Directly from a College or University	Direct Benefit to Agency in-house research	Substantial Involvement
Non-Funded Cooperative Agreement (NFCA)	Describing Research Work with No Obligation of Funds	Direct Benefit to Agency in-house research	Substantial Involvement
Technology Transfer Cooperative Research and Development Agreement (CRADA)	Receiving Funds under Federal Technology Transfer Act	Direct Benefit to Agency in-house research	Substantial Involvement
Reimbursable or Trust Fund Agreement	Agency Receives Funds to Perform Research Work	Direct Benefit to Agency in-house research	Substantial Involvement

Through these agreements, ARS researchers have received grants from state and national beekeeping and honey organizations to conduct work relevant to honey bee health, and ARS has funded these organizations to encourage large-scale, participatory research. ARS laboratories also have longstanding agreements with the beekeeping industry and commodity groups to test hypotheses and technologies in working apiaries and to share biological material. Cooperative Research and Development Agreements (CRADA) allow Federal agencies and private companies to work together to develop, scale, and market new technologies, such as improved pest-control systems (Box 1). ARS also works with peer institutions to help train the next generation of pollinator scientists. For instance, the ARS bee lab in Logan, UT, partners with the American Museum of Natural History to offer "THE BEE COURSE", [13] an annual nine-day workshop on bee taxonomy for botanists, conservation biologists, pollination ecologists, and other scientists.

USDA also provides grants for external research through NIFA. Several NIFA programs offer opportunities to fund research related to honey bee health, and to train the next generation of honey bee researchers. For instance, competitive, peer-reviewed research grants administered by NIFA's Agriculture and Food Research Initiative (AFRI) and Specialty Crop Research Initiative (SCRI) offer funding to qualified scientists and educators for research programs, education, and extension that could be relevant to honey bee health. The Sustainable Agriculture Research and Education (SARE) program has a long and ongoing

12. http://www.ars.usda.gov/Main/docs.htm?docid=16581
13. http://www.amnh.org/our-research/invertebrate-zoology/bee-course-2016/

Box 1: Developing New Miticides

Through a Cooperative Research and Development Agreement (CRADA), USDA-ARS and the company BetaTec tested the effectiveness of hops beta acids—a byproduct of processing hops for beer—on interrupting the lifecycle of the Varroa mite. This collaboration ultimately led to the development of HopGuard©, a natural miticide for control of the Varroa mite. HopGuard© is now commercially available to beekeepers.

Box 2: Volunteer help in pollinator research

The Smithsonian's Transcription Center recruits volunteers to help make cultural heritage and biodiversity data more accessible. In 2015-2016, volunteers working on the Center's "Bumblebee Project" transcribed label information from 44,000 bumblebee specimens, which had been digitized in 2014 during a Smithsonian Rapid Capture Pilot Project. This information on when and where each bee was collected helps scientists understand historical changes in the distribution of bumblebee species.

Photo: Smithsonian Institution

history of working with partners to support pollinator research, education, and publications. And NIFA's Small Business Innovation Research program has been used for several honey bee health concepts by providing funding for small businesses developing new technologies. Other USDA agencies, such as the Animal Plant Health Inspection Service (APHIS) and the Farm Service Agency (FSA), have entered a limited number of honey bee-focused assistance agreements.

USDA and other Federal agencies work with external associations[14] and participating stakeholders who share the interest in honey bees, pollinator services, beekeepers, and production agriculture. Here, Federal agencies and the private sector work together to improve honey bee health, identify solutions to health challenges, improve communication among participants, and bring science to improve decision-making.[15] Federal agencies also engage citizen scientists to advance pollinator research. For instance, in collaboration with non-governmental organizations (NGOs), the Department of the Interior (DOI) has opened some of the land it oversees to a number of citizen-science projects—like the annual BioBlitz,[16] which calls on citizens to help survey the biodiversity of different areas. The Smithsonian Institution has also worked through its Transcription Center to recruit volunteers to digitize its pollinator collection (Box 2).

---

14. E.g., American Honey Producers Association http://www.ahpanet.com/; American Beekeeping Federation http://www.abfnet.org/

15. For example, the Honey Bee Health Coalition brings together a consortium of beekeepers, researchers, growers, government agencies, agribusiness, conservation groups, and manufacturers. http://honeybeehealthcoalition.org/

16. http://nationalgeographic.org/projects/bioblitz/

Box 3: A pollinator plan for every state

To respond to the decline in honey bee colonies, many states and tribes are working with EPA, the State FIFRA Issues Research and Evaluation Group, and the Tribal Pesticide Program Council to draft Managed Pollinator Protection Plans (MP3s). The MP3s will enhance communication among growers, beekeepers, and pesticide applicators and set out best management practices for minimizing impacts of human activities, such as agriculture, on pollinator health while maintaining economic growth. Scientists from EPA and USDA-ARS often serve as technical experts in the development of these plans.

Monitoring and Extension

USDA agencies provide funding to a variety of university partners to conduct monitoring, outreach, and extension around bee health. NIFA funds a collaborative of leading researchers and extension specialists on a project called the Bee Informed Partnership (BIP[17]) to better understand the reasons behind honey bee losses. The BIP project developed a National Management Survey, building on an annual survey done in collaboration with the Apiary Inspectors of America and ARS scientists. This survey asks beekeepers to track colony losses and factors associated with these losses. With technical assistance from universities, ARS, and BIP, APHIS funds the annual National Survey of Honey Bee Pests and Diseases, monitoring the presence of diseases and invasive pests in apiaries across the United States. APHIS, ARS, and NIFA also provide financial and technical support to assist BIP in providing extension resources for beekeepers, and in coordinating data on honey bee health. BIP's Tech Transfer teams provide critical, real-time health assessments of hives, allowing beekeepers across the country to make timely and informed management decisions. NIFA also partners with Cooperative Extension and the eXtension.org website to maintain an online community[18] where land-grant universities and ARS work together to provide the most current scientifically-based beekeeping information and a forum for expert advice.

In response to the Presidential Memorandum, the National Agricultural Statistics Service (NASS) has now instituted enhanced national, statistically-based, quarterly and annual surveys of beekeepers to document honey bee colony mortality rates and insights into causes.[19] The high response rate from beekeepers to this comprehensive survey highlights the mutual benefits of a close relationship between a trusted government source and the agricultural sector it serves. In 2016, NASS will build on the honey bee mortality data by conducting the first-ever Cost of Pollination survey to track the cash fees associated with honey bee pollination of crops.

17. https://beeinformed.org/
18. http://articles.extension.org/bee_health
19. https://www.nass.usda.gov/Surveys/Guide_to_NASS_Surveys/Bee_and_Honey/

Risk Assessment and Pesticide Management

The Environmental Protection Agency (EPA) frequently works with universities, external organizations, and other non-Federal entities to collect data and conduct research to inform the regulation of pesticides and other products that may have harmful effects on honey bees and other pollinators. For example, the Federal Insecticide, Fungicide and Rodenticide Act (FIFRA) Scientific Advisory Panel (SAP) and the Pesticide Program Dialogue Committee (PPDC) engage outside experts and stakeholders to inform the EPA in evaluating risks and regulatory policy related to pesticides and pollinators. EPA also works with institutions outside of the United States. In 2014, the EPA collaborated with Health Canada and the California Department of Pesticide Regulation to release a harmonized guidance for assessing the risks that pesticides pose to bees.[20] In addition, EPA has been working with its regulatory counterparts worldwide (through the "Organisation for Economic Co-operation and Development" (OECD)) to develop study protocols for measuring bee toxicity and exposure to pesticides and associated impacts on bee health. EPA is also working with Canada's Pest Management Regulatory Agency (through the bilateral Regulatory Cooperation Council) and the California Department of Pesticide Regulation on a pesticide re-evaluation process for three neonicotinoid pesticides, and is working with the U.S.-Canada Regulatory Cooperation Council and the North American Free Trade Agreement Technical Working Group on Pesticides to incorporate pollinator-health considerations into scientific reviews of pesticides conducted by the United States, Canada, and Mexico. EPA also coordinates with domestic co-regulators through avenues including the State FIFRA Issues Research and Evaluation Group, the Association of American Pesticide Control Officials, and the Tribal Pesticide Program Council (Box 3).

Floral Resources

Honey bees require natural floral resources—with minimal exposure to agrochemicals and pollutants—to supplement their agricultural diets, as proper nutrition has positive effects on honey bee health that increase resilience to other known stressors. Multiple Federal agencies work with beekeepers to provide bees with access to forage on public lands. Federal land-management agencies—including the U.S. Army Corps of Engineers (Army Corps), the Bureau of Land Management (BLM), the Bureau of Reclamation

---

Box 4: Bringing bees to public lands

The U.S. Army Corps of Engineers (Corps) is known best for building and maintaining our country's infrastructure. But the Corps has also been a leader in providing homes for bees. In Fiscal Year 2015, the Corps worked with 22 beekeepers to host 1,364 hives (about 36 million bees) on its managed lands, and helped spread awareness of the importance of pollinator health through nearly 200 interpretive programs. The Corps also maintains more than 16,000 acres of pollinator habitat and nearly 300 pollinator gardens, partnering with other Federal agencies and citizen groups.

Photos: Ryan Hartwig, USACE; U.S. Fish and Wildlife Service

(USBR), the U.S. Fish and Wildlife Service (USFWS), and the U.S. Forest Service (USFS)—allow beekeepers to apply for special use permits to operate apiaries on multiple-use Federal lands (Box 4). Land manag-

20. https://www.epa.gov/pollinator-protection/pollinator-risk-assessment-guidance

ers assess each permit application for appropriateness based on the parameters of the beekeeping operation as well as the purpose of the land parcel.

Federal agencies also encourage and support the availability of floral resources for honey bees through conservation incentive programs, as discussed below (Focus Area 3: Land Conservation, Restoration, and Enhancement).

Partnership Priorities

In addition to nurturing and growing existing partnerships, Federal agencies are working to build new partnerships in priority areas to further accelerate progress in the improvement of honey bee health. Some of these are described in more detail below.

Research

The Pollinator Research Action Plan (2015) provides a guide to Federal pollinator-research priorities and opportunities, many of which are conducive to partner involvement. Partnerships to explore technology transfer are particularly fertile ground for collaboration. Germplasm development and bee breeding are two of the active areas of research that require industry participation to transfer laboratory methodology to the field. ARS and APHIS plan to continue this partnership with beekeepers and commodity groups to conduct research that is relevant to the honey bee industry. Partnerships with specific commodity organizations also hold promise for troubleshooting bee-health issues in ways that are highly relevant to the agricultural industry. One such example is the recently launched ARS bee research worksite in Davis, CA, which works closely with the California almond, apple, cherry, and pear boards. Another is the ARS bee laboratory

> **Box 5: Applied bee-research partnerships**
>
> The ARS Pollinating Insects Lab in Logan, UT, partners with the National Alfalfa Forage Alliance (NAFA) to set up cooperative agreements with researchers working on applied alfalfa pollination topics, leveraging the expertise of ARS and the alfalfa industry to guide research priorities.
>
>
>
> Photo: USDA image gallery, alfalfa leafcutter bee

in Logan, UT, which collaborates with the National Alfalfa Forage Alliance to examine the nexus between alfalfa and pollinators (Box 5). While continuing to nurture these and other current relationships, ARS is examining the potential for replicating these models and establishing new research partnerships at its other laboratories. There are also opportunities for NASS to partner with honey bee interest groups, state apiarists, and extension agents to encourage further participation in the new NASS Honey Bee Colony Health and Cost of Pollination surveys, mentioned above, which will provide rigorous data and analysis on the state of the honey bee industry.

Education and Outreach

Farmers and ranchers can support honey bee health by managing their land for honey bee forage and using pesticides in ways that avoid harm to honey bees and other beneficial insects. USDA is exploring opportunities with non-Federal entities to develop outreach materials on these topics for USDA Farm Service Agency (FSA) and the Natural Resources Conservation Service (NRCS) field offices to distribute to growers. These opportunities could include partnerships with state Integrated Pest Management (IPM) Programs and regional IPM centers to develop outreach materials on honey bee and pollinator-friendly pest management, tailored to the unique crop and pest issues facing different areas. USDA is also working with non-Federal entities on broader education and outreach efforts related to the health of honey bees and other pollinators, such as public service video announcements featuring celebrities who deliver information about pollinator biology and conservation. NIFA extension programs, State Agricultural Extension Agencies, and local/county extension offices provide valuable services to farmers, schools, community organizations such as 4-H, and individuals, such as the Agriculture In the Classroom (AITC)[21] program.

Land Access for Beekeepers

There are several ways in which partnerships can help expand land access for beekeepers. Federal landholding agencies can work with beekeeping organizations to clarify and advertise the process for requesting apiary access to multi-use Federal lands. Private landholding individuals and corporations can also work with these organizations to provide beekeepers with access to forage on their lands, and to improve the quality of forage available. Additionally, public and private incentive programs can provide cost-sharing opportunities for pollinator habitat. Federal agencies can work with non-Federal entities to promote Federal voluntary cost-share programs for pollinator habitat, as well as tax benefits that may be available to private landowners who make their land available to beekeepers. The American Bee Project, for instance, already provides state-by-state resources and advice for receiving tax benefits from beekeeping on private land. In addition to these types of collaborations designed to raise awareness of opportunities for extending land access for beekeepers, partnerships that provide technical assistance or support demonstration projects may be useful in ensuring that people actually take advantage of such opportunities.

---

21. https://nifa.usda.gov/program/agriculture-classroom-aitc-program

Focus Area 2: Monarch Butterfly Conservation

Introduction

The monarch butterfly is one of the best-known butterflies in North America. It has recently suffered serious population declines, raising the possibility that we will lose this iconic Continental migration.[22] The 2014–2015 overwintering count of 56.5 million butterflies for the Eastern monarch population was the second-lowest count on record, representing a population decline of 82% from the 20-year average.[23] As of 2014, the Western monarch population had declined by an estimated 50% from its previous average.[24] 2015-2016 Eastern migration numbers ~150 million butter-

> ### Box 6: Working Together to Plant Monarch Butterfly Habitat
>
> Youth organizations like Boy Scouts of America, Girl Scouts, and 4-H have a long history of working to educate youth and contribute to community well-being. Here, work is underway on a BSA Hornaday Award for wildlife conservation and habitat protection, by planting milkweed/milkflower in a community park to improve monarch butterfly habitat. Signage is critical to message the benefits of wildlife habitat to a broader audience, in this case contributing to the efforts of Monarch Watch and adding one more count to the Million Pollinator Garden Challenge.

flies occupying 10 acres of overwintering habitat, a result of optimal weather conditions during the breeding and migration cycle but countered somewhat by a late storm in the overwintering forests in Mexico, highlighting the tenuous nature of natural phenomena. The exact reasons for monarch declines—and ways to reverse—remain under investigation, but habitat loss and changes in agricultural practices and land use have contributed to less availability of *Asclepias spp.* (aka milkweed or milkflower, the obligate plant for monarch butterfly breeding) and other plants on which pollinators depend. Partnerships can address these stressors, helping to restore monarch populations (Box 6).

Past and Ongoing Partnerships

Research

Developing effective solutions to the problem of declining monarch populations requires further investigation into the causes of these declines and to identify priority areas for habitat conservation. In 2014, the U.S. Geological Survey (USGS) established the Monarch Conservation Science Partnership (MCSP)—a partnership among Federal agencies, university researchers, and non-government organiza-

---

22. Semmens et al. 2016. Quasi-extinction risk and population targets for the Eastern, migratory population of monarch butterflies (Danaus plexippus). Scientific Reports 6:23265. http://www.nature.com/articles/srep23265

23. https://www.whitehouse.gov/sites/default/files/microsites/ostp/Pollinator%20Health%20Strategy%202015.pdf

24. http://www.fs.fed.us/wildflowers/pollinators/Monarch_Butterfly/documents/ConservationMonarchNatureServeXercesSocietyJan2015.pdf

tions—to support research in both of these areas.[25] The MCSP concluded that, given a range of plausible thresholds, the population migration has a substantial probability of extinction given current trends. Conserving the monarch migration will require active management to reverse population declines, and the establishment of a population-size goal that is sufficient to buffer against future environmentally-driven variability. Efforts are underway to expand this science partnership beyond U.S. boundaries to include Mexico and Canada.

Engagement in citizen-science projects provides additional opportunities for the Federal government to work with non-Federal entities to advance understanding of monarch populations. Through these projects, citizen volunteers—often with the guidance of expert Federal employees—collect data on monarch populations and pests, helping researchers to investigate monarch threats and track recovery.[26] Federal agencies are working with the Monarch Joint Venture to develop a Monarch Butterfly Integrated Monitoring project that will help bring together the data and efforts of these citizen science programs into one ongoing snapshot of the monarch population size and distribution. This effort is being expanded into a continent-wide, shared, monitoring effort working with Canada and Mexico through the Trinational Monarch Conservation Science Partnership.

Habitat Conservation and Restoration

Effective monarch habitat enhancement and restoration requires participation from a variety of landowners, including home gardeners, managers of transportation rights-of-way, businesses, farmers, and ranchers. Federal agencies are working with non-Federal entities to expand monarch habitat on the properties of these landowners. USDA-NRCS is working with NGOs and the native seed industry to expand seed supplies for various species of milkweed, an essential food source for monarch caterpillars and nectar source for adults. With leadership from pollinator experts, the USDA-NRCS Plant Materials Program selects regionally-appropriate milkweed species, grows a stock of that species, and then transfers the stock to private seed producers who can propagate the seeds on a commercial scale. In addition, some Federal grant opportunities, such as the NRCS Conservation Innovation Grants and the NIFA-supported Sustainable

---

Box 7: Growing enough milkweed to go around

Restoring the health of monarch butterfly populations in the United States requires large supplies of native milkweed seeds. There are 73 species of native milkweeds in the United States. Through Project Milkweed, the USDA-NRCS Los Lunas Plant Materials Center has teamed up with the Xerces Society and private seed companies to test several milkweed species for commercial production. USDA is helping to develop initial stocks of seeds for these species, as well as best practices for growing and processing, which private industry can then use to develop commercial stocks. The USDA-NRCS Conservation Innovation Grant program has funded some of the Project Milkweed trial runs in commercial operations.

---

25. http://www.umesc.usgs.gov/management/dss/monarch.html
26. For examples of monarch butterfly citizen science activities, see: http://www.fs.fed.us/wildflowers/pollinators/Monarch_Butterfly/citizenscience/index.shtml

Agriculture Research and Education program, provide money to support partnerships in developing stocks, distributing, and planting seeds of pollinator-friendly plants (Box 7). Recognizing the need for a more coordinated approach to ensuring reliable supplies of genetically appropriate seed for restoration projects, Federal agencies, working with their non-Federal partners through the Plant Conservation Alliance, have developed a National Seed Strategy (NSS).[27] The NSS identifies specific objectives and actions under four goals (identifying seed needs and ensuring seed availability, identifying and conducting research, developing decision support tools, and developing communication strategies), all of which are focused on the NSS vision of providing the "right seed in the right place at the right time."

Federal agencies can increase monarch habitat on private lands through voluntary, incentive-based, conservation programs. NRCS launched the Monarch Butterfly Habitat Development Project, which provides financial and technical assistance to landowners through Farm Bill conservation programs to increase monarch habitat in ten states along the monarch migration route. During development of the project, NRCS and USFWS worked together to identify priority areas and conservation practices that would provide the greatest benefit for monarchs. The USFWS Partners for Fish and Wildlife Program also provides financial and technical assistance to landowners for private lands conservation and is focusing program resources on monarch conservation in priority areas, as part of the USFWS monarch conservation initiative.

In addition to collaborative efforts led by the Federal government, non-Federal entities play a critical role in organizing public and private partners, generating funding resources, and setting priorities for monarch-habitat restoration. The Monarch Joint Venture (MJV[28]) brings together Federal and state agencies, non-governmental organizations, and academic programs to support and coordinate monarch conservation efforts across the United States, under a steering committee that includes participation from the BLM, USDA, USFWS, and state fish and wildlife agencies. MJV funds efforts targeted at monarch habitat restoration and enhancement, such as the development of guides for planting monarch habitat, the creation of an integrated pest management framework for growing milkweeds, and on-the-ground planting projects. Several Federal agencies provide funding and/or in-kind support for MJV

> **Box 8: Giving monarchs the right-of-way**
>
> Power lines, roadsides, and other transportation rights-of-way (ROW) that are planted with pollinator-friendly vegetation can provide substantial, continuous habitat for monarchs and other pollinators, while saving land managers maintenance money. With funding from Federal agencies, the Monarch Joint Venture has been working with the Tallgrass Prairie Center to propagate milkweed seeds and plant them on highway roadsides in Iowa, through Iowa's Integrated Vegetation Management Program.

---

27. http://www.blm.gov/wo/st/en/prog/more/fish__wildlife_and/plants/seedstrategy.html
28. www.monarchjointventure.org

Box 9. One million pollinator seed packs

In 2015, W. Atlee Burpee and Company partnered with USDA and DOI to donate and distribute one million Bee Garden and Butterfly Brigade seed packets to educators, organizations, and home gardeners across the nation, including at the 2015 White House Easter Egg Roll. These packets included seeds for two species of milkweed, among other pollinator-friendly nectar plants. The distribution of these seed packets supported the Million Pollinator Garden Challenge (see "Focus Area 3: Pollinator Habitat).

projects. In another notable effort, the National Fish and Wildlife Foundation (NFWF) partnered with BLM, USDA, and USFWS to establish the Monarch Butterfly Conservation Fund in 2015. The fund accepts public and private contributions, as well as matching contributions from grantees, to fund monarch-conservation projects, with priority on habitat restoration and native-seed production. In 2015, the Fund awarded nearly $3 million in grants to conservation groups and agencies for 22 restoration and seed supply projects, leading to a total of $10 million being spent on monarch conservation.

To better engage and coordinate with the agricultural sector, Federal agencies have joined with industry and NGOs in forming a collaborative focused specifically around monarch conservation and agriculture. The Keystone Monarch Collaborative[29] is a group of organizations spanning the research community, agricultural production, conservation, and public agencies working to identify how partnerships in the farming and ranching community can support and enhance habitat for a sustainable monarch population. Universities also recognize the central importance of agricultural landscapes to monarch recovery efforts, with several North Central Land Grant Institutions launching a Rapid Response Program in 2015 to enhance habitat management in rural landscapes, in concert with productive agricultural practices. This NIFA-supported collaboration[30] will facilitate a coordinated research and science-based extension effort tailored to local farming and ranching conditions to complement citizen-led efforts in urban and suburban landscapes.

State fish and wildlife agencies and the Association of Fish and Wildlife Agencies (AFWA) are key leaders and partners in monarch conservation. At least 29 states have included monarchs in their State Wildlife Action Plan revisions, with 19 states and the District of Columbia noting it as a Species of Greatest Conservation Need. Many of the states in the central flyway are developing individual state strategies that engage a diverse set of state-based partners and Federal agencies in targeted planning and actions.

Federal agencies are also cooperating with international counterparts to ensure that sufficient monarch habitat is maintained across the entire migration routes of the Eastern and Western monarch populations in North America (Box 8). Through the Trilateral Committee for Wildlife and Ecosystem Conservation and Management, the USFWS is working with Canada and Mexico to protect monarchs by enhancing and

29. https://www.keystone.org/our-work/agriculture/monarch-collaborative/
30. http://www.nimss.org/projects/view/mrp/outline/17476

protecting habitat along monarch migration routes. This builds on the 2007 North American Monarch Conservation Plan[31] published by the Commission for Environmental Cooperation (CEC).

Education and Outreach

Education and outreach partnerships are important in raising awareness of the threats facing monarch butterflies, and in encouraging individuals and organizations to take steps—such as planting milkweed and butterfly gardens—to help reverse monarch declines. USFWS teamed with the MJV to develop and host Webinar series[32] on monarch biology, monitoring, and conservation through the National Conservation Training Center. Webinars cover a wide variety of topics, including fundamentals of habitat conservation, new research findings, and tips for supporting monarchs in urban settings. Agencies have also partnered with domestic and international NGOs to produce education and outreach materials targeted at younger audiences, and with local education groups and schools to open public lands to activities that teach students about biology and other topics while advancing monarch conservation.

Partnership Priorities

Habitat Conservation and Restoration

Availability of milkweed and nectar plants along the monarch migration route is critical to the recovery of monarch populations, particularly in the Midwestern prairie corridor. Federal agencies and offices can support this goal by engaging in collaborations to grow, distribute, and plant milkweed seeds and plugs. This includes increasing the economic feasibility of milkweed production by improving techniques for seed collection, processing, and germination, as well as pest-management methods, for various milkweed species. Efforts can include working with plant nurseries and commercial stores to enhance the availability of native plants suitable for pollinators, including the absence of pesticide residues that may be toxic to these insects. Federal agencies can also support habitat goals by continuing to form partnerships that promote the incorporation of milkweed and other pollinator-friendly species into gardening programs and habitat-restoration plans (Box 9).

Education and Outreach

The monarch butterfly is a charismatic species with broad appeal across nations and demographics, making it a strong candidate for education and outreach. Federal agencies will continue to work with non-Federal entities to raise the visibility of the plight of the monarch butterfly, as well as public awareness of the very tractable solutions to increasing the monarch population through habitat restoration and enhancement. There are opportunities for agencies to leverage their staff expertise and communication networks to amplify partner efforts to promote gardening, landscaping, and restoration for monarchs and other pollinators. For instance, USDA's People's Garden Initiative has established partnerships resulting in the establishment of more than 1,800 gardens worldwide, including a number of pollinator gardens. USDA can work with partners to establish more of these gardens as monarch demonstration projects, and as part of NIFA's extension programs. Public-private partnerships to engage the agricultural community are particularly important, as monarch habitat has suffered steep declines in rural areas.

---

31. http://www3.cec.org/islandora/en/item/2350-north-american-monarch-conservation-plan-en.pdf
32. http://nctc.fws.gov/topic/online-training/webinars/monarch-conservation.html

Focus Area 3: Pollinator Habitat: Land Conservation, Restoration, and Enhancement

The ways in which land is managed and used impact both managed and wild pollinators. As noted earlier, honey bees require floral resources to supplement their diets obtained while providing agricultural pollination services. Wild pollinators, such as native and other non-apis bees, moths, butterflies, birds, and bats, also require diverse floral resources, as well as other habitat features necessary to their life-cycle, such as nesting sites and places to lay eggs. To support pollinator health, Federal agencies should take advantage of opportunities to partner with non-Federal entities to study pollinator habitat requirements and support habitat creation, restoration, and enhancement efforts.

Past and Ongoing Partnerships

Private Land Conservation Programs

Private land conservation programs enable the Federal government to partner with private landowners to restore and enhance land for pollinators. These mutually beneficial programs provide financial incentives for landowners who implement and maintain conservation practices on their property for extended periods of time. Incentives may include annual rental payments, easements, cost-share programs, and/or other incentive payments for land devoted to conservation, as well as technical assistance and equipment to support implementation of the conservation practice. Some programs offer additional monetary bonuses at enrollment or additional weight in the competitive enrollment process to landowners who propose implementing conservation practices that support pollinator habitat.

USDA-FSA and USDA-NRCS both offer private land conservation programs—the Conservation Reserve Program (CRP), the Environmental Quality Incentives Program (EQIP), and the Conservation Stewardship Program (CSP)—that support the provision of habitat and forage for managed and wild pollinators on private land. NRCS sets the practice specifications and provides the technical expertise on execution for both FSA and NRCS programs: for instance, NRCS State Technical Committees develop seed specifications for CRP, EQIP, and CSP pollinator habitat to ensure dietary diversity, bloom availability across seasons, and compatibility with other conservation goals. NRCS has worked with NGOs

> **Box 10: Conservation brain trust**
>
> The 2014 Farm Bill provided for Pheasants Forever to employ 100 "Farm Bill Biologists" dedicated to assisting with CRP enrollment and delivering technical assistance. These biologists are co-located at USDA offices. In regions of the United States critical to honey production, Farm Bill Biologists are working to reverse the trend of declining CRP enrollment and encouraging landowners to select seed mixes that benefit pollinators.

Box 11. States leading the way for pollinators

The Texas Parks and Wildlife Department (TPWD) oversees the country's longest-standing Landowner Incentive Program (LIP). In partnership with USFWS, the National Fish and Wildlife Foundation, and others, the TPWD LIP is funding and managing restoration projects. In their 2015 call for proposals, TPWD placed an emphasis on supporting projects that benefit pollinator species.

to develop state and regional guides to incorporating pollinators into conservation practices, capitalizing on partners' entomological expertise. FSA, with input from private partners, is developing a honey bee-specific CRP practice to provide affordable, nutritious forage. USDA has also partnered with NGOs to co-locate biologists who are specially trained to achieve conservation outcomes through private land conservation programs (Box 10). In 2014, FSA focused efforts on a five-state initiative in the upper Midwest to increase sign-ups for pollinator habitat through the CRP,[33] and created an option to allow participants to receive additional payments to help improve habitat for pollinators. In 2016, NRCS developed a ten-state Monarch Habitat Development Project, with anticipated expansion in upcoming years.[34]

The USFWS Partners for Fish and Wildlife Program ("Partners Program") provides financial and technical assistance, plants, seeds and other materials for restoration projects, working one-on-one with landowners throughout the project development and implementation process to meet shared conservation objectives. The Partners Program engages landowners, Federal and state agencies, tribes, counties, cities, soil and water conservation districts, NGOs, businesses, and schools to identify and help deliver conservation priorities, including pollinator habitat. State fish and wildlife agencies also work with private landowners, through voluntary incentive programs, to implement habitat restoration and enhancement projects benefiting pollinators (Box 11).

Table 2 provides additional detail on Federal conservation incentive programs at DOI and USDA.

33. http://www.nrcs.usda.gov/wps/portal/nrcs/detail/national/plantsanimals/pollinate/?cid=stelprdb1263263
34. http://www.nrcs.usda.gov/wps/portal/nrcs/detail/national/plantsanimals/pollinate/?cid=nrcseprd402207

Table 2: Federal conservation incentive programs

Implementing Agency	Program	Description
DOI	Partners for Fish and Wildlife Program	Provides technical and financial assistance to private landowners and tribes who are willing to work with USFWS and other partners on a voluntary basis to help meet the habitat needs of Federal Trust Species. The program can assist with projects in all habitat types that conserve or restore native vegetation, hydrology, and soils associated with imperiled ecosystems.
DOI	Coastal Program	Provides financial and technical assistance to land managers and a diversity of conservation partners for the restoration and protection of coastal habitats on private and public lands throughout the nation.
USDA	Conservation Reserve Program	Pays a yearly rental payment in exchange for farmers removing environmentally-sensitive land from agricultural production and planting species that will improve environmental quality.
USDA	Conservation Reserve Enhancement Program	An offshoot of the Conservation Reserve Program, targets high-priority conservation issues identified by local, state, or tribal governments or non-governmental organizations. In exchange for removing environmentally-sensitive land from production and introducing conservation practices, farmers, ranchers, and agricultural land owners are paid an annual rental rate. Participation is voluntary, and the contract period is typically 10–15 years, along with other Federal and state incentives as applicable per each CREP agreement.
USDA	Environmental Quality Incentives Program	Provides financial and technical assistance to agricultural producers to plan and implement conservation projects that help animal populations and/or improve soil, water, plant, air and related natural resources on agricultural land and non-industrial private forestland.
USDA	Conservation Stewardship Program	Provides payments to improve and maintain existing conservation practices and undertake additional practices on working lands.
USDA	Regional Conservation Partnership Program	Promotes coordination between NRCS and its partners by using partnership agreements to deliver conservation assistance to producers.
USDA	Agricultural Conservation Easements Program	Provides financial and technical assistance to help conserve agricultural lands and wetlands and their related benefits.
USDA	Forest Legacy Program	Supports state efforts to protect environmentally-sensitive forest lands. The voluntary program focuses on the acquisition of partial interests in privately-owned forest lands and helps states develop and carry out their forest conservation plans. The program encourages and supports acquisition of conservation easements that restrict development, require sustainable forestry practices, and protect other values.
USDA	Forest Stewardship Program	Encourages long-term stewardship of important state and private forest landscapes. The program provides landowners with the professional planning and technical assistance they need to keep their land in a productive and healthy condition. Assistance offered through the FSP also provides landowners with enhanced access to other USDA conservation programs, forest certification programs, and forest product and ecosystem service markets. Special attention is given to landowners in landscape areas identified by State Forest Action Plans and those new to, or in the early stages of, managing their land in a way that embodies multi-resource stewardship principles.
USDA	State Acres for Wildlife Enhancement	Provides technical and financial assistance to eligible land owners and operators to address priority wildlife issues.

Citizens Helping on Federal Lands

In addition to sponsoring pollinator habitat on private lands, Federal agencies can also benefit from citizens helping on Federally-managed lands. National Public Lands Day (NPLD[35]) is the Nation's largest single-day volunteer effort to improve public lands across the country. Occurring annually in September, NPLD volunteers remove invasive plants, maintain trails, plant trees and pollinator forage, and remove rubbish on public lands in all 50 States, the District of Columbia, and Puerto Rico. In 2015, nearly 200,000 volunteers and park visitors celebrated NPLD, keeping the promise of the Civilian Conservation Corps that worked from 1933-1942 to preserve and protect America's natural heritage. Opportunities are not just limited to NPLD, with Federal agencies increasingly planting pollinator gardens on their grounds in response to the Presidential Memorandum, often with the support of local partners who donate their time to install the habitat. These actions follow new guidance issued in October 2014 by the Council on Environmental Quality[36] and the General Services Administration[37] that empower all Federal agencies to plant pollinator gardens at their facilities.

Home, School, Business, and Community Garden Programs

Large landholders are not the only ones with the ability to support pollinator habitat. Gardens, homes, schools, businesses, and other properties can all provide important pollinator habitat in urban and suburban landscapes. In June 2015, with the support of the White House Office of Science and Technology Policy, and in conjunction with the spring harvest of the White House Kitchen Garden,[38] the National Pollinator Garden Network launched the Million Pollinator Garden Challenge,[39] a public-private campaign to register online a million gardens and landscapes to support pollinators across the United States (Box 12).

Box 12: A Zoo in Your Own BackYard: Joining the Million Pollinator Garden Challenge

In 2015, First Lady Michelle Obama launched the Million Pollinator Garden Challenge, an effort to plant a million gardens to support the President's Pollinator Strategy. The MPGN is an unprecedented collaboration of garden clubs, environmental groups, industry trade associations, and Federal agencies to plant and register a million public and private gardens and landscapes to support pollinators. Everybody can be part of this Challenge, bringing life and species diversity to gardens across the Nation.

---

35. http://www.publiclandsday.org/

36. https://www.whitehouse.gov/administration/eop/ceq/sustainability/landscaping-guidance

37. GSA P100 Building Standards, Landscape Prescriptive Requirements, S. 2 5.5. Pollinators. http://www.gsa.gov/portal/mediaId/127494/fileName/P100_2016.action

38. https://www.whitehouse.gov/the-press-office/2015/06/02/first-lady-michelle-obama-harvest-white-house-kitchen-garden-highlight-p

39. http://millionpollinatorgardens.org/

Box 13: Bringing pollinators into road design

Native roadside plantings, and the ecological services they provide, are receiving more attention from roadway designers, thanks to a partnership between the USFS and the Federal Highway Administration (FHWA). These partners have created tools to incorporate native re-vegetation into overall road design and construction in the Pacific Northwest. The two agencies are now working to expand these resources for use in other parts of the nation. In addition to providing needed forage for pollinators, incorporating native vegetation does a great job of stabilizing soils, decreasing the spread of invasive plants, enhancing aesthetics, and improving ecosystem health. Through the partnership, USFS provides technical expertise, consultation, on-the-ground training, and information on plant materials to support FHWA native-vegetation projects.

Photo: U.S. Forest Service

Integrated Vegetation Management for Pollinator Habitat

Another way in which Federal agencies are working towards pollinator-health goals is by engaging in partnerships to support integrated vegetation management (IVM) along rights-of-way (ROW), such as along roadsides or under power lines where low vegetation is mandated for safety and access purposes. IVM is generally defined as the practice of promoting desirable, stable, low-growing plant communities—that will resist invasion by tall-growing tree species—through the use of appropriate, environmentally-sound and cost-effective control methods. Strategic IVM along ROWs can promote pollinator habitat while reducing maintenance costs. For instance, BLM, EPA, USFS, USFWS, and the National Park Service (NPS) have agreed to an MOU with the Edison Electric Institute (EEI) to cooperatively develop and implement IVM practices along Federally-managed powerline ROWs, in order to increase pollinator and wildlife habitat. In December 2015, the White House Office of Science and Technology Policy (OSTP) and the U.S. Department of Transportation hosted a summit with State Departments of Transportation (DOTs) to explore case studies and best practices related to the use of Integrated Roadside Vegetation Management (IRVM) and the installation of pollinator habitat along roadsides (Box 13).

Research

Supporting pollinators through land conservation, restoration, and enhancement requires research and monitoring to understand the impacts that land-management decisions have on pollinator species, as well as the effect of restoration and enhancement on their recovery. Federal agencies engage with a variety of non-Federal entities to carry out this work.

The U.S. Geological Survey, for example, collects data that measure the impact of conservation incentive programs on pollinator health, inventories pollinator diversity, models species distribution, and assesses the economic value of pollinator conservation programs, among other functions. In doing so, USGS works closely with Federal, state, NGO, and academic partners. The USGS John Wesley Powell Center for Analysis and Synthesis, in particular, serves as a hub of collaboration among government and academic scientists, offering funding, space, and computer-processing power for complex projects. The

Monarch Conservation Science Partnership's integrated monitoring strategy includes pilot projects for effectiveness monitoring at restoration sites. Similarly, USDA works closely with other entities to monitor and assess private land conservation programs. Partners generate both internal and public-facing documents that guide the implementation and revision of conservation policies relevant to pollinators. USDA-FSA is currently working with Federal and NGO partners on several assessment projects on CRP land, targeted at understanding the impact of the CRP on bee health and pollinator diversity.

Public Outreach

Farmers and ranchers have considerable capacity to increase pollinator habitat, as do small landholders and gardeners who can play an important role by providing urban and suburban habitat. Several Task Force agencies maintain robust educational programs and expansive educational material distribution networks.[40] Federal agencies will work with private partners to develop and distribute educational materials on the positive role that citizens can play in pollinator health through planting gardens, capitalizing on partners' subject matter expertise as well as their distribution networks (Box 14). The Million Pollinator Garden Challenge is one example of an outreach effort that can benefit greatly from public-private partnerships. Federal agencies are also working with private foundations and media outlets on pollinator conservation-themed films and public-service announcements, leveraging the expertise of engaged scientists, land managers, and educators with the visual magic of communications experts.[41]

Partnership Priorities

Conservation Programs on Private Lands

The acreage dedicated to pollinator habitat on private lands can benefit from increased participation in voluntary conservation programs. To encourage enrollment, Federal agencies can work with non-Federal entities to advertise the availability of these

> **Box 14: Building pollinator habitat abroad**
>
> The Department of State is working with the National Wildlife Federation at embassies and consulates around the world—like the U.S. Mission in Geneva, Switzerland, pictured below—to make embassy and consulate facilities wildlife-friendly by converting manicured landscaping to native plants that are rich with floral resources for pollinators and other wildlife.

---

40. http://www.nrcs.usda.gov/wps/portal/nrcs/detail/plantmaterials/technical/publications/?cid=stelprdb1044847
http://www.fs.fed.us/wildflowers/pollinators
http://www.fws.gov/pollinators/Index.html
https://www.nps.gov/subjects/pollinators/index.htm
https://www.environment.fhwa.dot.gov/ecosystems/vegmgmt_pollinators.asp
https://www.epa.gov/pollinator-protection
https://qrius.si.edu/explore-science/jump/precious-pollinators

41. For example, National Geographic's NatGeo WILD Honey Bee documentary http://files.natgeonetworks.com/sQXw0L-zJ-nu4R and The Incredible Story of the Monarch Butterfly https://www.youtube.com/watch?v=zR5AljGZfjM; and the forthcoming Tree Media Foundation Pollinator Series in partnership with USDA.

programs, particularly directed toward areas where pollinator resources are low but demand is high. Examples of these areas include natural forage to support over-summering honey bees in the upper Midwest, and pollinator habitat along the prairie plains States to support the migration of the Eastern population of the monarch butterfly. Organizations with strong networks in these and other priority regions can greatly assist the Federal government in achieving pollinator-health goals. Federal agencies can also work with non-Federal entities to communicate to stakeholders how conservation programs that do not focus primarily or solely on pollinators can nevertheless deliver benefits to pollinators. This can leverage the unique knowledge of local and regional organizations to train agency field staff in installing and maintaining pollinator habitat on public and private lands in urban, suburban, and rural settings.

Best Management Practices

The development and availability of scientifically-vetted best management practices (BMPs) is key to enabling land managers to restore and enhance pollinator habitat. These BMPs include approaches for planting and maintaining pollinator habitat, integrated vegetation management (IVM), and integrated pest management (IPM) practices to minimize harm to pollinators from pesticide use. In addition to Federal BMPs developed in response to the President's Memorandum,[42] a number of non-government organizations also provide critical pollinator guidance.[43] Federal agencies can work with academic institutions and NGOs to develop and promote such practices, and with regional and local partners to tailor these practices to the particular geographies and considerations of individual land managers. For instance, the NIFA Sustainable Agriculture Research and Education (SARE) program offers grants for research and education focused on promoting agricultural innovation and providing "train the trainer" courses designed to teach participants about pollinator health. These courses include requirements, pollinator-friendly farm-

> **Box 15: Developing pollinator-specific management practices**
>
> Although USDA's private land conservation programs have always included best management practices, until recently, none of these practices were targeted specifically at supporting pollinator health. USDA-FSA has been working with scientists at the Pollinator Partnership to understand the benefits of pollinator-specific practices to manage honey bees and native pollinators, and to improve and encourage land managers to adopt such practices.

ing practices, approaches for habitat enhancement, and how to take advantage of resources offered by private land conservation programs to support pollinator health. Federal agencies can also work with partners to assess the efficacy of current best management practices as well as to develop improved ones (Box 15).

---

42. See footnotes 5 – 8 above
43. Pollinator Partnership Eco-Regional Planting Guides http://www.pollinator.org/guides.htm
   Xerces Society, Pollinator Friendly Plant Lists http://www.xerces.org/pollinator-conservation/plant-lists/

Expanding Pollinator Habitat along Rights-of-Way

Rights-of-Way offer tremendous potential to expand habitat and create corridors of movement for pollinators, while minimizing maintenance costs, supporting low-height vegetation, enhancing aesthetic appeal, and taking pressure off lands assigned to other productive purposes. There are numerous ways in which partnerships can help expand pollinator habitat along ROWs, including: joint efforts between Federal land-management agencies and utilities to support pollinator habitat on utility ROWs that pass through Federally-managed lands; between Federal natural-resource agencies and Federal, state, and local transportation agencies to support pollinator habitat along roadsides and other transportation ROWs; and between Federal agencies and NGOs to conduct education and outreach efforts to raise awareness of the benefits of non-traditional ROW maintenance and additional resources to supplement government funding.

Congress has recently legislated in support of pollinators on transportation ROWs in the 2015 Fixing America's Surface Transportation (FAST) Act. Section 1415 specifically highlights the enhancement of habitat and forage for pollinators as an eligible expense for Federal highway projects, and directs USDOT to promote integrated vegetation management practices and the development of

> ### Box 16: Creating an Interstate-35 "Monarch Highway"
>
> Serendipitously, the annual monarch butterfly migration, from winter retreats in the Oyamel forests in Mexico, northward across the United States to Canada, and returning in Fall, centers on a broad path across the prairies that parallels Interstate-35. The six State Departments of Transportation that manage I-35 – Texas, Oklahoma, Kansas, Missouri, Iowa, and Minnesota – with the Federal Highway Administration, have agreed to work together and with external funding organizations to support pollinator habitat along this "Monarch Highway," messaging the theme of pollinator habitat restoration broadly to counties and States critical to this iconic annual migration.
>
>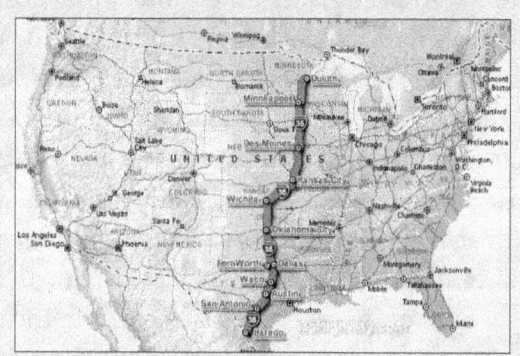
>
> *Diagram: White House Office of Science and Technology Policy*

habitat and forage for monarch butterflies, other native pollinators, and honey bees. FHWA has since issued a memorandum to its field staff on Improving Habitat for Pollinators[44] in response to this legislation. One exemplary opportunity to establish and expand pollinator habitat is along the Interstate-35 corridor—the "Monarch Highway" (Box 16)—where the six State DOTs with management and maintenance responsibilities for I-35 (TX, OK, KS, MO, IA, MN) are working with Federal agencies and NGOs to leverage pollinator habitat opportunities. These include increasing highway roadside habitat, but more importantly to communicate with adjacent communities and States on their prairie heritage and the broad opportunities to restore pollinator and prairie habitat. This and other transportation habitat projects offer a promising collaborative pathway to identify and implement further beneficial uses of rights-of-way.

---

44. https://www.environment.fhwa.dot.gov/ecosystems/vegmgmt_pollinators_improving_habitat.asp